Sinus Diet

A Beginner's 5-Step Guide to Managing Sinusitis Through Diet, With Sample Recipes and a Meal Plan copyright © 2023 Brandon Gilta

All rights reserved No part of this book may be reproduced, or stored in a retrieval system, or transmitted in any form or by any means, electronic, mechanical, photocopying, recording, or otherwise, without express written permission of the publisher.

Disclaimer

By reading this disclaimer, you are accepting the terms of the disclaimer in full. If you disagree with this disclaimer, please do not read the guide.

All of the content within this guide is provided for informational and educational purposes only, and should not be accepted as independent medical or other professional advice. The author is not a doctor, physician, nurse, mental health provider, or registered nutritionist/dietician. Therefore, using and reading this guide does not establish any form of a physician-patient relationship.

Always consult with a physician or another qualified health provider with any issues or questions you might have regarding any sort of medical condition. Do not ever disregard any qualified professional medical advice or delay seeking that advice because of anything you have read in this guide. The information in this guide is not intended to be any sort of medical advice and should not be used in lieu of any medical advice by a licensed and qualified medical professional.

The information in this guide has been compiled from a variety of known sources. However, the author cannot attest to or guarantee the accuracy of each source and thus should not be held liable for any errors or omissions.

You acknowledge that the publisher of this guide will not be held liable for any loss or damage of any kind incurred as a result of this guide or the reliance on any information provided within this guide. You acknowledge and agree that you assume all risk and responsibility for any action you undertake in response to the information in this guide.

Using this guide does not guarantee any particular result (e.g., weight loss or a cure). By reading this guide, you acknowledge that there are no guarantees to any specific outcome or results you can expect.

All product names, diet plans, or names used in this guide are for identification purposes only and are the property of their respective owners. The use of these names does not imply endorsement. All other trademarks cited herein are the property of their respective owners.

Where applicable, this guide is not intended to be a substitute for the original work of this diet plan and is, at most, a supplement to the original work for this diet plan and never a direct substitute. This guide is a personal expression of the facts of that diet plan.

Where applicable, persons shown in the cover images are stock photography models and the publisher has obtained the rights to use the images through license agreements with third-party stock image companies.

Table of Contents

Introduction	8
What Is Sinusitis?	11
Types of Sinusitis	11
Causes of Sinusitis	12
Symptoms of Sinusitis	13
Risk Factors of Sinusitis	15
Medical Treatments for Sinusitis	17
Lifestyle Changes to Manage Sinusitis	18
The Role of Supplements and Herbs in Sinus Health	20
What Is Sinusitis Diet?	22
Principles of Sinusitis Diet	22
Benefits of Sinusitis Diet	24
Disadvantages of Sinusitis Diet	28
5-Step Guide to Get Started with Sinusitis Diet	33
Step 1: Understanding the Sinusitis Diet	33
Step 2: Planning Your Meals	34
Step 3: Smart Grocery Shopping	36
Step 4: Preparing Your Food Correctly	37
Step 5: Monitoring Progress and Making Adjustments	38
Foods to Eat	40
Foods to Avoid	41
Sample Meal Plan	43
Day 1	43
Day 2	43
Day 3	44
Day 4	44
Day 5	44
Day 6	45
Day 7	45

Sample Recipes   47
- Oatmeal with Blueberries and a Drizzle of Honey   48
- Turkey Wrap   49
- Baked Cod   50
- Lentil Salad   51
- Grilled Salmon   53
- Chicken and Vegetable Stir-Fry   55
- Grilled Chicken Salad   57
- Quinoa Salad   59
- Lemon Ginger Tea   61
- Garlic Stir Fry   62
- Broccoli Stir Fry   64
- Berry Smoothie   66
- Seafood Soup with Leafy Greens   67
- Pineapple Salsa   69
- Spicy Chicken Soup   70
- Turmeric Ginger Soup   71
- Pineapple-Banana Smoothie   73

Conclusion   74

FAQs   77

References and Helpful Links   79

Introduction

Are you frequently battling with sinusitis, those persistent and bothersome symptoms that seem to take a toll on your day-to-day life? The headache, the nasal congestion, the facial pain—it can all become overwhelming. But what if I told you there's a way to manage these symptoms and even reduce their occurrence through a simple yet effective solution—your diet?

Sinusitis is a common condition affecting millions of people worldwide. It could be acute, lasting for a few weeks, or chronic, persisting for more than 12 weeks despite treatment attempts. While medication is often the first line of defense, an often-overlooked aspect is the role of diet in managing and preventing sinusitis.

A well-planned sinusitis diet guide can be a powerful tool in your fight against this condition. It involves consuming foods that help boost your immune system and reduce inflammation while avoiding those that trigger congestion and mucus production.

Just imagine being able to breathe freely again, without the constant pressure around your nose and eyes. Imagine going through your day without worrying about sudden bouts of coughing or sneezing. It seems like a dream, doesn't it? But it doesn't have to be.

Following this carefully crafted Sinusitis Diet Guide could be your reality. You would not only be aiding your body in fighting off the infection but also improving your overall health, leading to a better quality of life.

In this guide, we will talk about the following:

- What is Sinusitis?
- Types of Sinusitis
- Symptoms, causes, and risk factors of Sinusitis
- When to Seek Medical Attention
- Medical Treatments for Sinusitis
- Lifestyle Changes to Manage Sinusitis
- What is a Sinusitis Diet?
- Principles, benefits, and disadvantages of Sinusitis Diet
- 5-Step Guide to Get Started with Sinusitis Diet
- Foods to Eat and to Avoid

So, are you ready to take control of your health and bid farewell to the incessant sinusitis symptoms? Keep reading as we delve deeper into this guide, exploring the different foods to include in your diet and those to avoid, backed by scientific research. Let's take this journey together towards a healthier, happier you.

In the forthcoming sections, we will discuss how certain foods can influence your sinus health, tips to modify your diet effectively, and how to maintain this new dietary lifestyle. With this guide, you're not just tackling sinusitis; you're taking an essential step towards holistic wellness.

What Is Sinusitis?

Sinusitis, often referred to as a sinus infection, is a common condition where the lining of the sinuses becomes inflamed. This inflammation usually occurs after a cold or an allergic attack. The inflammation can block the sinuses, leading to a buildup of mucus and causing symptoms like pain, nasal congestion, and a reduced sense of smell. In some cases, it can also lead to fever, fatigue, and a cough that may worsen at night.

Types of Sinusitis

Sinusitis, also known as sinus infection, is an inflammation or swelling of the tissue lining the sinuses. It can be classified into several types based on its duration and the nature of the symptoms.

Acute Sinusitis: This is the most common type. It lasts for up to 4 weeks and is often caused by a common cold, allergies, or environmental triggers. Symptoms include facial pain or pressure, nasal stuffiness, nasal discharge, loss of smell, and cough or congestion.

Subacute Sinusitis: This type of sinusitis lasts for 4 to 12 weeks. It's often a continuation of acute sinusitis that hasn't fully resolved.

Chronic Sinusitis: If symptoms persist for 12 weeks or longer despite medical treatment, it's referred to as chronic sinusitis. It's characterized by prolonged sinus inflammation and recurring sinus infections.

Recurrent Sinusitis: This refers to several attacks within a year. People with recurrent sinusitis have several bouts of acute sinusitis in a year.

Each type of sinusitis has similar symptoms but they require different treatment approaches. If you suspect you have sinusitis, it's important to seek medical advice for appropriate diagnosis and treatment.

Now that we have a better understanding of sinusitis let's explore the causes and risk factors associated with it.

Causes of Sinusitis

Sinusitis, a common condition affecting many people worldwide, can be triggered by various factors:

Common Cold: This viral infection often inflames and blocks the sinuses, leading to acute sinusitis. Symptoms typically include a stuffy nose and headache.

Allergies: Allergic reactions can cause an inflammation of the sinus tissue. The swelling can block the sinuses, leading to symptoms such as pressure in the forehead and cheeks.

Nasal Polyps: These are small growths in the nasal passages that can block the sinuses or nasal passage, causing chronic sinusitis. They may lead to a decreased sense of smell and facial pain.

Deviated Nasal Septum: This is a condition where the thin wall between your nostrils is displaced to one side. A severe deviation can block the sinus passages, leading to frequent infections and sinusitis.

Immune System Disorders: Certain disorders like HIV or conditions that weaken the immune system can increase the risk of sinusitis due to a reduced ability to fight infections.

By understanding the underlying causes, you can modify your diet to reduce inflammation and boost your immune system, contributing to a healthier sinus lining.

Symptoms of Sinusitis

The symptoms of sinusitis can vary depending on the type and severity of the condition. Some common signs and symptoms include:

Nasal Congestion: This symptom involves a blocked or stuffy nose, which can interfere with sinus drainage and make breathing through the nose difficult.

Facial Pain/Pressure: Sinusitis often results in discomfort or a feeling of fullness in the face, especially around the forehead, eyes, and cheeks.

Loss of Smell and Taste: Inflammation and blockages can disrupt the sense of smell and taste, leading to these senses being diminished or lost entirely.

Headache: The inflammation and pressure in the sinuses can often cause pain in the forehead, temples, and sometimes the back of the head.

Cough or Throat Irritation: As the discharge from your sinuses drains down the back of your throat, it can cause irritation and a persistent cough.

Fatigue: Chronic sinusitis can often lead to a persistent feeling of tiredness or fatigue, affecting one's energy levels and overall well-being.

Fever: While not as common, some people with sinusitis may experience a fever as their immune system fights off the infection.

If you're experiencing any of these symptoms, consult a medical professional for an accurate diagnosis. Once confirmed, making dietary changes can help alleviate your symptoms and improve your overall health.

Risk Factors of Sinusitis

Now that we've shed light on the common symptoms of sinusitis, it's essential to identify the risk factors associated with the condition. The risk factors include the following:

Dental Infection: An infection in the teeth can spread to the sinuses, causing inflammation and blockage. This creates a conducive environment for bacteria to grow, leading to sinusitis.

Fungal Infection: Fungi are common in our environment and a fungal infection can cause an inflammation in the sinuses, resulting in sinusitis.

Exposure to Pollutants: Regular exposure to pollutants like cigarette smoke or industrial air pollution can damage the cilia (tiny hair-like structures) in the sinuses that help move mucus out. This can lead to sinusitis.

Mucus Blockage: Sinusitis often occurs when there is a blockage in the openings of your sinuses, usually caused by excessive mucus or swelling of the nasal tissue.

Maxillary Dental Pain: Pain in the upper jaw and teeth is a common symptom of sinusitis. It's caused by pressure from inflamed and swollen sinuses.

Hay Fever or Allergies: Allergies can cause the tissues in the nose to swell and produce more mucus, leading to sinusitis.

Common Cold: A common cold can inflame and block the sinuses, making them a perfect breeding ground for bacteria, which can result in sinusitis.

Nasal Abnormalities: Any problem inside the nose, such as a deviated septum or nasal polyps, can block the sinus openings and lead to sinusitis.

Seasonal Allergies: Like hay fever, seasonal allergies can cause inflammation in the sinuses and increase mucus production, triggering sinusitis.

Genetic Factors: Certain genetic factors can make some people more susceptible to conditions like chronic rhinosinusitis. These individuals often have an overactive immune response to fungi, which can lead to long-term sinus inflammation.

Knowing these risk factors can help you take preventative measures to reduce your chances of developing sinusitis.

Medical Treatments for Sinusitis

The treatment for sinusitis depends on the type, severity, and underlying cause of the condition. Here are some common medical treatments that your doctor may recommend:

Antibiotics: These are used to treat sinusitis that's thought to be caused by bacteria. The antibiotics help kill the bacteria, allowing the body to heal.

Corticosteroids: These are often used as a nasal spray and can help reduce inflammation in the nasal passages, improving symptoms of sinusitis.

Decongestants: These medications help narrow the blood vessels and reduce swelling in the lining of the nose, making breathing easier while your body fights off the infection.

Pain Relievers: Over-the-counter pain relievers can be used to manage the discomfort associated with sinusitis. They're typically used to relieve headaches, facial pain, and other discomforts.

Immunotherapy: If allergies are contributing to your sinusitis, allergy shots (immunotherapy) might improve your condition by reducing the body's reaction to specific allergens.

Surgery: In cases where sinusitis is chronic or doesn't respond to other treatments, surgery may be an option to clear the sinuses and restore normal function.

By consulting a medical professional, they can determine the best course of treatment for your specific case. However, in addition to these treatments, making dietary changes and adopting lifestyle habits may also help improve your symptoms.

Lifestyle Changes to Manage Sinusitis

Aside from medical treatments, making simple lifestyle changes can also help alleviate symptoms of sinusitis and improve your overall health. These include the following:

Hydration: Drinking plenty of fluids helps to thin out the mucus and drain the sinuses. This can reduce symptoms and prevent sinusitis from worsening.

Healthy Diet: Eating a balanced diet boosts the immune system, making it easier to fight off infections that can lead to sinusitis.

Regular Exercise: Regular physical activity can help improve circulation and boost the immune system, which can reduce the risk of sinusitis.

Quit Smoking: Smoke and other pollutants can irritate the sinuses and cause inflammation, increasing the risk of sinusitis. Quitting smoking can significantly reduce this risk.

Limit Alcohol: Alcohol can cause swelling in the nasal and sinus tissues, leading to inflammation and increased mucus production. Limiting alcohol intake can help manage sinusitis symptoms.

Use a Humidifier: Dry air can irritate the sinuses. Using a humidifier adds moisture to the air and can help soothe inflamed sinuses.

Manage Allergies: If allergies are causing sinusitis, managing them with antihistamines or allergy shots can help control sinusitis symptoms.

Avoid Cold and Flu: Frequent hand washing and avoiding close contact with people who have colds or the flu can reduce the risk of developing sinusitis.

Adequate Rest: Getting enough sleep is crucial for the body's ability to heal and resist infections, helping to prevent and manage sinusitis.

Nasal Irrigation: Regular use of saline nasal sprays or washes can help keep the nasal passages moist and clear of mucus, reducing sinusitis symptoms.

These lifestyle changes can not only help alleviate symptoms of sinusitis but also improve your overall health and prevent future episodes. It's essential to work with your doctor to determine the best combination of treatments and lifestyle changes for your specific condition.

The Role of Supplements and Herbs in Sinus Health

Supplements and herbs can play a significant role in promoting sinus health. They can help to reduce inflammation, boost the immune system, and alleviate symptoms associated with sinusitis. Here are some beneficial supplements and herbs:

Quercetin

Quercetin is a flavonoid found in many fruits and vegetables. It has anti-inflammatory and antihistamine effects that can help reduce sinus congestion. A common dosage recommendation for quercetin is between 500-1000mg per day, taken in two divided doses. However, it's always best to consult your healthcare provider before starting any new supplement regimen.

Bromelain

Bromelain is an enzyme found in pineapples. It's known to reduce swelling in the nasal passages and relieve sinus pressure, making it beneficial for those suffering from sinusitis. For sinus issues, a typical dose of bromelain is between 500-2000mg per day, divided into two or three doses. Again, it's crucial to consult your healthcare provider for personalized advice.

Echinacea

Echinacea is an herb often used to boost the immune system and fight infections. It can be particularly helpful in treating sinusitis. The dosage for echinacea can vary depending on the form (capsule, tincture, tea, etc.), so it's essential to follow the instructions on the supplement label.

Precautions

While these supplements and herbs can be beneficial, they're not without potential risks. Some people may experience side effects such as stomach upset, allergic reactions, or interactions with other medications. Therefore, always talk to your healthcare provider before starting any new supplement or herb regimen, especially if you're currently taking other medications or have underlying health conditions.

What Is Sinusitis Diet?

A sinusitis diet is a meal plan that focuses on incorporating specific foods and nutrients to help manage the symptoms of sinusitis. It aims to reduce inflammation, boost the immune system, and promote overall sinus health. While there is no specific "sinusitis diet," incorporating certain foods and avoiding others can have significant effects on managing and preventing sinusitis.

Principles of Sinusitis Diet

The principles of a Sinusitis Diet are based on boosting the immune system and reducing inflammation. Key principles include:

Hydration: Hydration not only helps thin out mucus in the sinuses but also facilitates its drainage, providing relief for sinusitis sufferers. Drinking plenty of fluids is therefore a crucial component of a sinusitis-focused diet, as it supports the body's natural processes of clearing and healing.

Avoid Certain Foods: The principle of a sinusitis diet is to avoid certain foods that can worsen sinus congestion. These foods can include dairy products, refined sugars, processed foods, and alcohol. By avoiding these trigger foods, individuals with sinusitis can help alleviate symptoms and promote overall sinus health.

Food Intolerance: Food intolerance is a crucial aspect of a sinusitis diet as it can alleviate the risk of sinus infections triggered by specific foods. Understanding one's intolerances and avoiding them can significantly improve overall sinus health. Paying close attention to symptoms and keeping a food diary can aid in identifying and avoiding potential triggers.

Antioxidant-Rich Foods: Antioxidants are vital nutrients for the body's immune system to combat the inflammation caused by sinusitis. These micronutrients complement the medication and alleviate the symptoms by reducing oxidative stress and free radical damage.

Reduce Refined Sugar and Fast Food: TReducing refined sugar and fast food is one of the primary principles of a sinusitis diet as it can impair the immune system's ability to fight off infections. Processed foods and sugary drinks can also lead to systemic inflammation, exacerbating sinusitis symptoms.

Each person's response to the diet may vary, so it's essential to monitor symptoms and adjust as necessary. As always, it's recommended to consult with a healthcare professional before making significant dietary changes.

Benefits of Sinusitis Diet

The Sinusitis Diet can offer several potential benefits, particularly for individuals struggling with chronic or recurrent sinusitis. Here are a few key benefits:

Reduced Inflammation

When sinus inflammation occurs, the result can be painful symptoms such as sinus congestion, headaches, and pressure. However, by following a proper diet plan, people can alleviate these symptoms.

A sinusitis diet focuses on reducing foods that can trigger inflammation while increasing the consumption of foods with anti-inflammatory properties. This dietary approach aims to reduce sinus inflammation and help manage sinusitis symptoms more effectively. By limiting pro-inflammatory foods, people can reduce inflammation in the nasal passages, allowing for easier breathing and less pressure in the sinuses.

Incorporating anti-inflammatory foods that contain high levels of antioxidants, vitamins, and minerals can also help enhance the body's immune system to fight against infections, thereby preventing future attacks of sinusitis. In addition to managing symptoms, following a sinusitis diet can provide long-term health benefits to one's overall well-being.

Improved Immune Function

A diet that is high in vitamins, minerals, and antioxidants is effective in improving the immune system's functions. Proper nutrition can help the immune system to better protect the body against potential threats, including bacteria and viruses that cause sinusitis, a common inflammatory condition that affects the sinuses.

Ensuring a diet rich in fruits, vegetables, and whole grains can provide the necessary nutrients to support optimal immune system function and help prevent sinusitis. Additionally, antioxidants like vitamins C and E and beta-carotene are vital in maintaining a healthy immune system as they can protect it from damage caused by free radicals.

As such, consuming a diet that is rich in antioxidants helps ensure optimal immune system function. By incorporating a diet that is rich in nutrients and antioxidants, individuals can be better equipped to fight off infections, including those that cause sinusitis.

Better Sinus Drainage

One of the primary benefits of a sinusitis diet is that it can aid in better sinus drainage, allowing you to breathe easier and prevent the development of sinusitis. Hydration is crucial for proper sinus function, as it helps keep the mucous membranes moist, making it easier for your body to expel mucus and other irritants.

Consuming mucus-thinning foods, such as chicken soup or hot tea with honey and lemon, can also help to unclog congested sinuses. Additionally, a sinusitis diet that is rich in vitamins and minerals, particularly those with anti-inflammatory properties, can help prevent the inflammation and swelling that contributes to sinusitis.

Less Frequent Flare-Ups

Following a sinusitis diet can offer individuals a range of health benefits, including fewer and less severe sinusitis flare-ups over time. This diet typically involves eating foods that are low in sugar, processed foods, and other allergens that can exacerbate sinusitis symptoms. As a result, individuals who adhere to this diet can expect to experience better overall sinus health and a reduction in related symptoms, such as congestion, headaches, and facial pressure.

It is important to note that while a sinusitis diet can be effective in managing symptoms, it should be used in conjunction with other treatments, such as medication, nasal irrigation, and allergy management. Additionally, those who suffer from severe or chronic sinusitis should consult with a healthcare professional before making significant changes to their diet or treatment plan.

Overall Health Improvement

By following a diet that is rich in water and essential nutrients, individuals suffering from sinusitis can significantly improve their overall health and well-being. Hydration is crucial to our body in many ways, including the regulation of body temperature, digestion, and transportation of nutrients. Drinking enough water not only prevents dehydration but also helps thin the mucus in the sinuses, making it easier to drain.

Moreover, nutrient-dense foods like fruits and vegetables are rich in vitamins and minerals, which play a vital role in strengthening the immune system, reducing inflammation, and preventing infections. A healthy diet can also reduce the risk of developing chronic health conditions such as heart disease, type-2 diabetes, and some cancers. Therefore, focusing on a diet that promotes hydration and nutrient-rich foods not only helps relieve sinusitis symptoms but also contributes to overall health improvement.

Remember, individual responses to dietary changes can vary widely, and what works well for one person might not work as well for another. It's always a good idea to consult with a healthcare provider when considering significant dietary changes.

Disadvantages of Sinusitis Diet

While the Sinusitis Diet can offer significant benefits, it's important to acknowledge some potential drawbacks. Here are a few:

Limited Food Choices

The restrictive nature of the sinusitis diet poses a significant challenge for meal planning and food choices. Given the need to avoid certain foods that trigger inflammation, individuals with sinusitis may find themselves limited in their selection of dishes that cater to their preferences and dietary needs. This limitation can be frustrating, especially for those who enjoy a wide range of cuisines or have preferences towards certain ingredients.

In addition, the reduced food choices may result in nutritional inadequacies, which can negatively impact one's overall health and well-being. Proper meal planning and guidance from healthcare professionals or nutritionists are essential to ensure that individuals on this diet can meet their nutritional requirements and maintain a balanced diet. Despite these challenges, the adoption of a sinusitis diet is widely recognized as an effective intervention to manage and alleviate the symptoms of sinusitis.

Initial Discomfort

During the initial period of adapting to a sinusitis diet, some individuals may experience discomfort due to sudden changes in their eating habits. A sinusitis diet is designed to reduce inflammation in the sinuses and promote healing. However, the sudden elimination of certain foods from the diet can cause temporary discomfort such as headaches, fatigue, or gastrointestinal upset.

This can be attributed to the body adjusting to the reduction of inflammatory ingredients, particularly processed and packaged foods, refined sugars, and dairy products. Additionally, as the body adapts to this new way of eating, there may be a temporary reduction in energy levels as the body begins to utilize fat stores instead of carbohydrates for energy.

Therefore, it is important to be patient and give the body ample time to adjust to this new lifestyle change. With perseverance and time, individuals can reap the benefits of a sinusitis diet, which include reduced inflammation, improved sinus function, and overall improved health and well-being.

Potential Nutrient Deficiencies

One of the main concerns when following a sinusitis diet is the potential for nutrient deficiencies. This is because many of the foods that need to be avoided are typically high in important vitamins and minerals. For example, citrus fruits are a common trigger for sinusitis symptoms and are therefore often avoided on the diet, but they are also an excellent source of vitamin C. This vitamin is essential for the immune system to function properly and for the body to absorb other important nutrients like iron.

Similarly, dairy products may be eliminated due to their potential to create excess mucus, but they are also an important source of calcium, which is necessary for strong bones and teeth. To avoid nutrient deficiencies, it is important to consume a variety of other nutrient-dense foods and to consult with a healthcare professional or registered dietitian to ensure that the diet is balanced and meets individual nutritional needs.

Time and Effort

One of the major disadvantages of following a sinusitis diet is the time and effort it requires to adhere to the diet's guidelines. Planning meals, shopping for specific foods, and preparing them can be a time-consuming and arduous process. Not only do individuals with sinusitis need to avoid certain foods that trigger inflammation and congestion, but they also need to incorporate foods that have anti-inflammatory properties.

This means including a variety of fruits, vegetables, whole grains, and lean proteins in their meals. Moreover, they need to be mindful of their salt intake, as excessive sodium can worsen sinus symptoms. The preparation of food also needs to be tailored to minimize allergens, irritants, and other triggers that can exacerbate sinusitis symptoms. In summary, while a sinusitis diet can provide significant relief to those experiencing chronic sinusitis, it may require significant time and effort to maintain.

Food Intolerance Identification

Food intolerance identification can be a complex and daunting process for people suffering from sinusitis symptoms. These symptoms can range from headaches, sinus pressure, and nasal congestion to even more severe conditions, such as chronic sinusitis and inflammation of the mucous membranes.

One of the most significant challenges of identifying food intolerances is that the symptoms of sinusitis can often be caused by a wide range of foods, making it difficult to pinpoint the exact culprit. Additionally, the symptoms of food intolerances may not be immediate, which further complicates the process of determining which foods to eliminate from one's diet.

Moreover, the elimination process can take several weeks or even months, and a limited diet can lead to nutritional deficiencies and a host of other health issues. Therefore, it is essential to work with a healthcare professional to determine the best approach for identifying and managing food intolerances.

However, despite these challenges, many find the benefits of the Sinusitis Diet far outweigh the drawbacks. The potential for reduced inflammation, improved immune function, better sinus drainage, fewer flare-ups, and overall health improvement makes the effort worthwhile for many individuals suffering from chronic or recurrent sinusitis. As always, it's crucial to consult with a healthcare provider before embarking on significant dietary change.

5-Step Guide to Get Started with Sinusitis Diet

Sinusitis is an uncomfortable condition that can cause pain, pressure, and congestion in your sinuses. One way to manage these symptoms is through a sinusitis diet, which involves eating foods that reduce inflammation and boost the immune system. This comprehensive guide will walk you through the steps to get started with a sinusitis diet.

Step 1: Understanding the Sinusitis Diet

Embarking on a sinusitis diet is an empowering step towards taking control of your health. This journey isn't about seeking quick fixes or temporary relief; it's about making impactful, long-term changes to your eating habits to boost your overall health and reduce sinusitis symptoms.

At its core, a sinusitis diet revolves around foods that are rich in anti-inflammatory properties and nutrients that supercharge the immune system. Picture your plate filled with colorful fruits and vegetables, brimming with antioxidants and vitamins that help your body fight inflammation. Envision lean proteins like chicken and fish, supplying you with essential amino acids for tissue repair and recovery. Imagine healthy fats from sources such as avocados and nuts, providing you with the necessary fuel for your day and supporting your body's natural inflammation response.

However, this new dietary lifestyle isn't just about what you should add to your meals, but also about what you need to limit or avoid. Processed foods, sugary snacks, and certain types of dairy products can be detrimental to your efforts. These foods often contain ingredients that trigger inflammation or weaken the immune system, potentially worsening your sinusitis symptoms.

Therefore, the secret to a successful sinusitis diet lies in finding the right balance. It's about embracing the consumption of foods that boost your health and wellbeing, while consciously limiting those that might exacerbate your sinusitis symptoms. This understanding is the first step towards creating a dietary plan that works for you, one that can guide you toward a healthier future free from the discomfort of sinusitis.

Step 2: Planning Your Meals

Now that you have a solid understanding of the sinusitis diet, it's time to put that knowledge into action. The next crucial step is meal planning, a process that ensures you're incorporating the right foods into your diet and steering clear of those that can trigger inflammation.

Think of meal planning as sketching a roadmap for your dietary journey. It's about deciding in advance what you'll eat for each meal throughout the week, ensuring your diet stays aligned with your health goals. This strategy involves making a list of all your meals, focusing on including a wide variety of fruits, vegetables, lean proteins, and healthy fats.

Consider using a meal planner or an app to keep track of your meals and ensure you're maintaining a balanced intake of nutrients. These tools can help you visualize your meals for the week and make adjustments as needed. They can also serve as a reminder of your commitment to healthier eating, helping you stay on track.

Remember, the ultimate goal here is to make food choices that contribute to your health and wellbeing, and that minimize sinusitis symptoms. By planning your meals, you can resist the temptation of convenient but unhealthy options, such as quick, processed foods. Instead, you'll be prepared with nutritious, homemade meals that align with your sinusitis diet.

Meal planning might seem daunting at first, but with time, it becomes a habit. And it's a habit that pays off, providing you with a clear path to follow in your quest for better health. So, grab a pen and start charting your course towards a sinusitis-friendly lifestyle today.

Step 3: Smart Grocery Shopping

Your meal plan is ready, and now it's time to bring it to life. The next essential step is grocery shopping. However, this isn't just about filling your cart; it's about making smart, informed choices that align with your sinusitis diet.

Remember, your focus should be on fresh produce, lean proteins, and healthy fats. Picture yourself selecting vibrant fruits and vegetables, teeming with the vitamins and antioxidants your body needs. Choose lean proteins like chicken or fish, which provide the essential amino acids for tissue repair and immune support. Don't forget to include sources of healthy fats like avocados or nuts, which are key for energy and inflammation control.

Conversely, you'll want to avoid processed foods, which often harbor hidden sugars and unhealthy fats. These ingredients can trigger inflammation and undermine your efforts toward managing your sinusitis symptoms. So, even if a food item is labeled as 'healthy' or 'low fat,' always take a moment to read the label. Look out for ingredients such as high fructose corn syrup, hydrogenated oils, or artificial preservatives, which are red flags for processed foods.

A helpful strategy is to shop mainly around the perimeter of the grocery store. This is typically where you'll find fresh foods—fruits, vegetables, meats, and dairy. The central aisles often house processed foods, so try to avoid these areas.

Grocery shopping for a sinusitis diet might require more time and attention than you're used to. But remember, every smart choice you make is a step towards better health. You're not just shopping; you're investing in your well-being. So, arm yourself with your meal plan, put on your reading glasses, and dive into the exciting world of smart grocery shopping. Your body—and especially your sinuses—will thank you for it.

Step 4: Preparing Your Food Correctly

The fourth step in your journey towards a healthier diet is all about preparing your food in a way that maximizes its nutritional value and minimizes potential inflammation. This means not only choosing the right foods but also paying attention to how you cook them.

Steaming, grilling, or roasting are recommended cooking methods for a sinusitis diet. These techniques allow the natural flavors of your food to shine through without the need to add unhealthy fats. For instance, grilling can bring out the sweetness in vegetables and the savory flavors in meats, while steaming helps preserve the nutrients in your food, ensuring you get the most health benefits from each bite.

But it's not just about how you cook your food; it's also about what you add to it. Incorporating anti-inflammatory spices like turmeric and ginger into your meals can add a burst of flavor and provide health benefits as well. These spices have been used for centuries in various cultures for their medicinal properties, including their ability to fight inflammation and boost the immune system.

Remember, the goal is to consume foods that promote overall health and alleviate sinusitis symptoms. That means opting for cooking methods that preserve the integrity of your ingredients and choosing seasonings that enhance both the taste and nutritional value of your meals.

Food preparation is an integral part of your sinusitis diet. It's where you have the opportunity to put your knowledge into practice and truly transform your ingredients into meals that nourish your body and help manage your sinusitis symptoms. So, dust off those pots and pans, and let's get cooking!

Step 5: Monitoring Progress and Making Adjustments

The final, but equally crucial step in the initiation of your sinusitis diet involves actively monitoring your progress and making necessary adjustments as you go. This isn't a one-size-fits-all approach, but rather a personalized journey towards better health.

Start by tuning into your body's responses after eating certain foods. Are there any immediate changes in how you feel? Do some foods seem to trigger or exacerbate your sinusitis symptoms? If you notice such a pattern, it might be best to eliminate these potential culprits from your diet. This isn't about restricting yourself, but instead about making choices that serve your well-being.

Keeping a food diary can also be an effective strategy. Jot down what you consume each day, along with any sinusitis symptoms you experience. Over time, you might start to see correlations between certain foods and your symptoms, helping you to tailor your diet more effectively.

In addition to self-monitoring, regular check-ins with a healthcare provider or nutritionist are highly recommended. These professionals can provide valuable insight into how well your diet is working for you. They can help assess your progress, identify any nutritional gaps, and suggest adjustments as necessary.

Remember, there's no rush. Modifying your diet is a significant lifestyle change, and it needs time to show results. Patience will be your ally in this process.

Starting a sinusitis diet is indeed a significant commitment. It demands understanding the diet, planning meals, smart grocery shopping, proper food preparation, and constant monitoring of progress. But with dedication, patience, and professional guidance, this diet can lead to substantial improvements in your sinusitis symptoms and overall health.

The journey to a healthier you starts with mindful eating. A sinusitis diet could be your key to managing your symptoms more effectively and improving your quality of life. So, embrace this opportunity to take control of your health, one meal at a time.

Foods to Eat

In a sinusitis diet, it's important to include foods that can help reduce inflammation and boost the immune system. Here are some of the foods you should consider:

Fruits and vegetables: They are rich in antioxidants and vitamins that can boost your immune system. Examples include citrus fruits like oranges and lemons which are high in vitamin C, and leafy green vegetables.

Omega-3 fatty acids: Foods rich in omega-3 fatty acids like fish, walnuts, and flaxseeds can help reduce inflammation.

Spicy foods: Spicy foods like chili peppers can help clear your sinuses.

Garlic and onions: These have powerful anti-inflammatory properties and can help fight off infection.

Ginger: This can help reduce inflammation and soothe sore throats.

Turmeric: It contains curcumin, a compound known for its anti-inflammatory effects.

Hydrating fluids: Drinking lots of water, herbal tea, or clear broths can help keep your mucus thin and help alleviate congestion.

Remember, everyone is different so it's important to pay attention to how your body reacts to different foods. If certain foods seem to worsen your symptoms, it may be best to avoid them.

Foods to Avoid

If you're dealing with sinusitis, certain foods can potentially worsen your symptoms. Here are some foods to avoid:

Dairy products: Dairy products like milk, cheese, and ice cream can increase mucus production and exacerbate congestion.

Processed foods: These foods are often high in sodium which can lead to fluid retention and worsen inflammation.

Refined sugars: Foods and drinks high in sugar can impair immune function and promote inflammation.

Fried and fatty foods: Fried and fatty foods should be avoided in a sinusitis diet as they can exacerbate symptoms. The consumption of such foods can lead to the production of excess mucus and inflammation in the nasal passages, aggravating the condition.

Caffeine: Caffeinated drinks like coffee and tea can dehydrate you, thickening your mucus and worsening symptoms.

Alcohol: Alcoholic beverages should be avoided in a sinusitis diet due to their dehydrating effects and ability to cause swelling in the nasal and sinus tissues. Additionally, the consumption of alcohol can worsen sinusitis symptoms, such as nasal congestion and headaches.

Certain fruits and vegetables: Some people find that certain fruits and vegetables, especially those high in histamine like tomatoes, spinach, and eggplant, can trigger or worsen sinusitis symptoms.

Remember, everyone's body is different and these are general recommendations. It may be helpful to keep a food diary to identify any specific food triggers for your sinusitis symptoms.

Sample Meal Plan

Here's a 7-day meal plan designed to reduce inflammation and mucus production—common symptoms of sinusitis. Please note this is just a guideline and individual dietary needs may vary.

Day 1

Breakfast: Oatmeal with blueberries and a drizzle of honey

Lunch: Grilled chicken salad with lots of leafy greens, cucumber, tomatoes, and olive oil dressing

Dinner: Grilled salmon with a side of steamed broccoli and quinoa

Snacks: A handful of almonds and carrot sticks

Day 2

Breakfast: Scrambled eggs with spinach and mushrooms

Lunch: Lentil soup with carrots, celery, and onions

Dinner: Baked turkey breast with sweet potato and green beans

Snacks: Fresh apple slices, celery sticks with hummus

Day 3

Breakfast: Smoothie made with banana, spinach, flaxseeds, and almond milk

Lunch: A salad consisting of quinoa, garnished with feta cheese crumbles, cucumber, and cherry tomatoes.

Dinner: Baked cod with a side of brown rice and asparagus

Snacks: An orange and a handful of walnuts

Day 4

Breakfast: Whole grain toast with avocado and a hard-boiled egg

Lunch: Chicken and vegetable stir-fry with brown rice

Dinner: Baked sweet potato stuffed with black beans, corn, and salsa

Snacks: Fresh strawberries and a handful of pumpkin seeds

Day 5

Breakfast: Oatmeal with sliced bananas and a sprinkle of cinnamon

Lunch: Wrap of turkey served in a whole grain tortilla, garnished with lettuce, tomatoes, and slices of avocado.

Dinner: Baked chicken with a side of sweet potato mash and green beans

Snacks: An apple and a handful of almonds

Day 6

Breakfast: Mixed berries and honey served with Greek yogurt.

Lunch: Tuna salad with lettuce, tomatoes, cucumber, and olive oil as dressing

Dinner: Quinoa and steamed zucchini served with grilled shrimp

Snacks: A banana and carrot sticks with hummus

Day 7

Breakfast: Smoothie made with blueberries, spinach, chia seeds, and coconut water

Lunch: Lentil salad with carrots, celery, and onions

Dinner: Grilled salmon with a side of brown rice and steamed broccoli

Snacks: Fresh orange slices and celery sticks with hummus

Remember to drink plenty of water throughout the day, and avoid foods that could potentially worsen your sinusitis symptoms.

Sample Recipes

In this chapter, we'll provide you with some simple and tasty recipes that are perfect for a Sinusitis-friendly diet.

Oatmeal with Blueberries and a Drizzle of Honey

Ingredients:

- 1 cup of oats
- 2 cups of water or milk (for creamier oatmeal)
- A pinch of salt
- 1 cup of fresh blueberries
- 1-2 tablespoons of honey

Instructions:

1. Pour the oats into a pot, and add the water (or milk) and a pinch of salt.
2. Heat the mixture over medium-high heat until it begins to boil. After it starts boiling, lower the heat and allow it to gently simmer. Stir from time to time for roughly 10 minutes, until the oats reach your preferred consistency.
3. Remove the pot from the heat and let the oatmeal sit for 2 minutes to continue to thicken.
4. Serve the oatmeal in a bowl, top with the fresh blueberries, and drizzle honey over the top.
5. Enjoy your healthy and delicious breakfast!

Feel free to adjust the amount of honey based on how sweet you like your oatmeal. You can also add other toppings like nuts or seeds for extra nutrition.

Turkey Wrap

Ingredients:

- 1 whole grain tortilla
- 3-4 slices of turkey breast
- 1 handful of lettuce
- 2-3 slices of tomato
- 1/2 ripe avocado
- Optional: mayonnaise, mustard, or your preferred condiment

Instructions:

1. Lay the whole-grain tortilla flat on a clean surface or plate.
2. Spread a thin layer of your chosen condiment (mayonnaise, mustard, etc.) on the tortilla.
3. Place the turkey slices in the center of the tortilla, leaving some space at the bottom for folding.
4. Add the lettuce on top of the turkey.
5. Arrange the tomato slices over the lettuce.
6. Slice the avocado and place it on top of the tomatoes.
7. Fold in the sides of the tortilla and then roll it up from the bottom to make a wrap.
8. Cut the wrap in half diagonally and serve.

Baked Cod

Ingredients:

- 4 cod filets
- 2 tablespoons lemon juice
- 2 tablespoons butter, melted
- 1/4 cup all-purpose flour
- 1/2 teaspoon salt
- 1/4 teaspoon paprika
- 1/4 teaspoon black pepper
- Lemon slices and fresh parsley for garnish

Instructions:

1. Preheat your oven to 400 degrees F (200 degrees C).
2. Place the cod filets into a baking dish. Drizzle with lemon juice and melted butter.
3. In a small bowl, combine the flour, salt, paprika, and black pepper. Sprinkle this mixture evenly over the cod filets.
4. Bake in the preheated oven for about 20 minutes or until the fish flakes easily with a fork.
5. Garnish with lemon slices and fresh parsley before serving.
6. Serve the baked cod with a side of brown rice and asparagus for a healthy, balanced meal.

Lentil Salad

Ingredients:

- 1 cup dry lentils
- 2 cups water
- 2 medium carrots, diced
- 2 celery stalks, diced
- 1 medium onion, finely chopped
- 3 tablespoons olive oil
- 2 tablespoons apple cider vinegar
- Salt and pepper to taste
- Fresh parsley, chopped (optional)

Instructions:

1. Rinse the lentils under cold water.
2. In a pot, bring the 2 cups of water to a boil.
3. Add the rinsed lentils to the boiling water, then reduce the heat to low, cover the pot, and let it simmer for about 20-25 minutes, or until the lentils are tender but not mushy.
4. While the lentils are cooking, dice the carrots and celery, and finely chop the onion.
5. Once the lentils are done, drain them and let them cool for a bit.
6. In a large bowl, combine the cooked lentils, diced carrots, celery, and chopped onion.

7. In a small bowl, whisk together the olive oil, apple cider vinegar, salt, and pepper to make a dressing.
8. Pour the dressing over the lentil mixture in the large bowl, then toss everything together until well coated.
9. If desired, sprinkle some chopped fresh parsley on top for extra flavor and color.
10. Enjoy your healthy and delicious Lentil Salad!

This can be served immediately, or you can let it chill in the fridge for a bit to let the flavors meld together.

Grilled Salmon

Ingredients:

- 4 salmon filets
- 2 tablespoons olive oil
- Salt, to taste
- Pepper, to taste
- Lemon slices, for garnish

For the marinade:

- 1/4 cup of soy sauce
- 1/4 cup of brown sugar
- 1/4 cup of water
- 1/4 cup of olive oil

Instructions:

1. First, make the marinade. In a small bowl, combine the soy sauce, brown sugar, water, and olive oil until the sugar dissolves.
2. Place the salmon filets in a dish and pour the marinade over them. Cover and marinate in the refrigerator for at least 2 hours.
3. Preheat your grill to medium heat.
4. Brush the grill with olive oil to prevent the salmon from sticking.
5. Remove the salmon from the marinade and place on the grill.

6. Grill each side for around 4-6 minutes, depending on the thickness of your salmon. The salmon should have a nice char and flake easily when it's done.
7. Season with salt and pepper to taste, and garnish with lemon slices before serving.
8. Serve the grilled salmon with a side of brown rice and steamed broccoli for a healthy, balanced meal.

Chicken and Vegetable Stir-Fry

Ingredients:

- 2 chicken breasts, cut into thin strips
- 2 cups mixed vegetables (like bell peppers, broccoli, carrots, snow peas)
- 1 tablespoon vegetable oil
- 2 cloves garlic, minced
- 1 tablespoon fresh ginger, grated

For the Sauce:

- 1/4 cup low-sodium soy sauce
- 1 tablespoon cornstarch
- 1 tablespoon honey
- 1 tablespoon sesame oil

Instructions:

1. Heat the vegetable oil in a large wok or skillet over medium-high heat.
2. Add the chicken strips and cook until no longer pink, about 5-7 minutes.
3. Add the garlic and ginger and stir for another minute.
4. Add the mixed vegetables and stir-fry until they are tender-crisp, about 5 minutes.
5. In a small bowl, whisk together the soy sauce, cornstarch, honey, and sesame oil.

6. Pour the sauce over the chicken and vegetables in the wok/skillet and stir well to coat.
7. Continue cooking for another 2-3 minutes, or until the sauce has thickened.
8. Serve the chicken and vegetable stir-fry with a side of brown rice or noodles for a complete meal.

Grilled Chicken Salad

Ingredients:

- 2 boneless, skinless chicken breasts
- Salt and pepper to taste
- 2 tablespoons olive oil
- 1 head of lettuce, washed and torn into bite-sized pieces
- 2 tomatoes, diced
- 1 cucumber, sliced
- 1/4 cup of red onion, thinly sliced
- 1/2 cup crumbled feta cheese
- Your choice of salad dressing

Instructions:

1. Preheat your grill to medium-high heat.
2. Season the chicken breasts with salt and pepper, then drizzle them with 1 tablespoon of olive oil.
3. Place the chicken on the grill and cook for 6-7 minutes per side, or until the internal temperature reaches 165 degrees Fahrenheit. Remove the chicken from the grill and let it rest for a few minutes.
4. While the chicken is resting, prepare your salad. In a large bowl, combine the lettuce, tomatoes, cucumber, red onion, and feta cheese.
5. Slice the grilled chicken into thin strips and add it to the salad.

6. Drizzle the salad with the remaining tablespoon of olive oil and your choice of salad dressing. Toss everything together until well combined.
7. Serve the salad immediately, while the chicken is still warm.

Quinoa Salad

Ingredients:

- 1 cup quinoa
- 2 cups water
- 1/4 cup extra-virgin olive oil
- 1 lime, juiced
- 2 teaspoons ground cumin
- 1 teaspoon salt
- 1/2 teaspoon red pepper flakes (optional)
- 1 1/2 cups halved cherry tomatoes
- 1 cucumber, diced
- 5 green onions, finely chopped
- 1/4 cup chopped fresh cilantro

Instructions:

1. Bring quinoa and water to a boil in a saucepan. Reduce heat to medium-low, cover, and simmer until quinoa is tender and water has been absorbed, 10 to 15 minutes. Set aside to cool.
2. In a large bowl, whisk olive oil, lime juice, cumin, salt, and red pepper flakes together to create the dressing.
3. In the bowl with the dressing, mix in quinoa, tomatoes, cucumber, and green onions. Stir until well mixed.
4. Top with cilantro and stir until everything is well combined.

5. You can serve it right away, or let it sit for a while to let the flavors meld together.

Lemon Ginger Tea

Ingredients:

- 1-inch piece of fresh ginger root
- 1 lemon
- 1-2 teaspoons of honey (optional)
- 2 cups of water

Instructions:

1. Peel the ginger root and slice it into thin slices.
2. Bring the water to a boil in a small pot or saucepan.
3. Once the water is boiling, add the ginger slices and reduce the heat to low, allowing it to simmer for about 10 minutes.
4. While the ginger is simmering, squeeze the juice from the lemon.
5. After 10 minutes, remove the ginger tea from the heat and add the lemon juice. Stir well.
6. If you'd like a sweet tea, add honey to taste at this point.
7. Strain the tea into a cup or mug.
8. Your Lemon Ginger Tea is ready to serve! Enjoy it hot for a soothing, refreshing drink.

Garlic Stir Fry

Ingredients:

- 2 tablespoons olive oil
- 4 cloves garlic, minced
- 1 bell pepper, sliced
- 1 onion, sliced
- 2 carrots, julienned
- 1 zucchini, sliced
- 2 tablespoons soy sauce (or to taste)
- Salt and pepper to taste

Instructions:

1. Heat the olive oil in a large pan or wok over medium heat.
2. Add the minced garlic to the pan and cook for about 1 minute until it becomes fragrant. Be careful not to burn the garlic.
3. Add the bell pepper, onion, carrots, and zucchini to the pan. Stir fry the vegetables for about 5-7 minutes, or until they are tender-crisp.
4. Pour the soy sauce over the vegetables, stirring well to ensure they are evenly coated.
5. Season with salt and pepper to taste.
6. Continue to stir fry for another 2-3 minutes, then remove from heat.

7. Your Garlic Stir Fry is ready to serve! This dish works well on its own, or as a side to grilled meats or fish.

Remember, you can customize your stir fry by adding any of your favorite vegetables or even some tofu or chicken for extra protein.

Broccoli Stir Fry

Ingredients:

- 1 large head of broccoli, cut into florets
- 1 red bell pepper, sliced
- 2 cloves of garlic, minced
- 2 tablespoons of olive oil
- Salt and pepper to taste
- Optional: 1 tablespoon of soy sauce or tamari for added flavor

Instructions:

1. Heat the olive oil in a large pan or wok over medium heat.
2. Add the minced garlic to the pan and sauté it until it becomes fragrant. This usually takes about a minute.
3. Add the broccoli florets and sliced red bell pepper to the pan. Stir everything together, making sure the vegetables are coated with the oil and garlic.
4. Cover the pan and let the vegetables cook for about 5 minutes, or until they are as tender as you like. Stir occasionally to ensure they don't burn.
5. Season the stir fry with salt and pepper to taste. If you're using soy sauce or tamari, add it now and stir well to make sure all the vegetables are evenly coated.

6. Once the vegetables are cooked to your liking and the seasonings have been thoroughly mixed in, remove the pan from the heat.
7. Serve your Broccoli Stir Fry hot, ideally with a side of brown rice or quinoa for a balanced meal.

Berry Smoothie

Ingredients:

- 1 cup of mixed berries (such as strawberries, blueberries, raspberries)
- 1 ripe banana
- 1 cup of almond milk or any other non-dairy milk
- Optional: 1 tablespoon of honey or maple syrup for added sweetness

Instructions:

1. Start by adding the almond milk to your blender.
2. Next, add in the ripe banana and your choice of mixed berries.
3. If desired, add a tablespoon of honey or maple syrup for extra sweetness.
4. Blend on high until everything is thoroughly mixed and the smoothie has a creamy consistency. This usually takes about a minute or two depending on your blender.
5. Pour your Berry Smoothie into a glass or a smoothie bottle if you're on the go.
6. Enjoy immediately for the freshest taste and to benefit from all the nutrients.

Seafood Soup with Leafy Greens

Ingredients:

- 1 cup of mixed seafood (shrimp, calamari, mussels)
- 2 cups of leafy greens (spinach, kale)
- 1 medium onion, finely chopped
- 2 cloves of garlic, minced
- 1 tablespoon of olive oil
- Salt and pepper to taste
- 4 cups of water or seafood broth
- Fresh herbs for garnish (optional)

Instructions:

1. Heat the olive oil in a large pot over medium heat.
2. Add the finely chopped onion, and sauté until it becomes translucent, which should take about 5 minutes.
3. Add the minced garlic to the pot and continue to sauté until the garlic is fragrant.
4. Add the mixed seafood to the pot. Cook until the seafood is fully cooked. This typically takes about 5-7 minutes but can vary based on the types of seafood you're using. The shrimp should be pink and the calamari should be white.
5. Add the water or broth to the pot and bring the mixture to a boil.

6. Once boiling, add the leafy greens to the pot. Reduce the heat to low and let the soup simmer for about 10 minutes, or until the greens have wilted and are tender.
7. Season the soup with salt and pepper. You can adjust these to taste.
8. Ladle the soup into bowls and garnish with fresh herbs if desired. Serve hot.

Pineapple Salsa

Ingredients:

- 1 cup fresh pineapple, diced
- 1/2 cup cucumber, diced
- 1/2 cup red onion, diced
- 1 jalapeno, seeds, and ribs removed, finely diced
- Juice of 1 lime
- Salt to taste
- Freshly chopped cilantro (optional)

Instructions:

1. In a large bowl, combine the diced pineapple, cucumber, red onion, and jalapeno.
2. Squeeze the juice of one lime over the mixture.
3. Add salt to taste and mix well.
4. If desired, add freshly chopped cilantro for an additional layer of flavor.
5. Let the salsa sit for about 10 minutes to allow the flavors to meld together.
6. Serve immediately with your choice of chips or as a topping for grilled chicken or fish.

Spicy Chicken Soup

Ingredients:

- 2 chicken breasts, skinless and boneless
- 1 tablespoon olive oil
- 1 onion, chopped
- 3 cloves garlic, minced
- 1 jalapeno pepper, seeded and chopped
- 1 red bell pepper, chopped
- 4 cups chicken broth
- 1 can (14.5 oz) diced tomatoes
- 1 teaspoon cayenne pepper
- Salt and black pepper to taste
- 2 tablespoons fresh cilantro, chopped

Instructions:

1. Heat the olive oil in a large pot over medium heat. Add the chicken breasts and cook until browned on both sides. Remove the chicken from the pot and set aside.
2. In the same pot, add the onion, garlic, jalapeno, and bell pepper. Cook until the vegetables are soft.
3. Cut the cooked chicken into bite-sized pieces and return it to the pot. Add the chicken broth, diced tomatoes, cayenne pepper, salt, and black pepper. Bring the soup to a boil, then reduce the heat and let it simmer for about 20 minutes.
4. Stir in the chopped cilantro just before serving.

Turmeric Ginger Soup

Ingredients:

- 2 tablespoons olive oil
- 1 onion, finely chopped
- 3 cloves garlic, minced
- 1 tablespoon fresh ginger, grated
- 1 teaspoon turmeric
- 1 cup carrots, chopped
- 1 cup celery, chopped
- 4 cups vegetable broth
- Salt and pepper to taste
- 2 tablespoons of lemon juice

Instructions:

1. Begin by warming the olive oil in a sizable pot over a medium flame. Proceed to incorporate the diced onion, crushed garlic, shredded ginger, and turmeric. Continue to sauté for roughly 5 minutes, or until the onions become see-through.
2. Add the chopped carrots and celery to the pot and continue to cook for another 5 minutes.
3. Pour in the vegetable broth and bring the soup to a boil.
4. Once boiling, reduce the heat and allow the soup to simmer for about 20 minutes, or until the vegetables are tender.

5. Season the soup with salt and pepper to taste, then stir in the lemon juice.
6. Serve hot.

Pineapple-Banana Smoothie

Ingredients:

- 1 cup fresh pineapple chunks
- 1 ripe banana
- 1 cup almond milk (unsweetened)
- 1 tablespoon honey
- A pinch of cayenne pepper (optional)

Instructions:

1. Pour almond milk into a blender, followed by ripe banana and pineapple pieces.
2. Blend until smooth and creamy.
3. Add the honey and blend again until it's well incorporated.
4. If you like a bit of spice and extra sinus-clearing power, add a pinch of cayenne pepper and stir well.
5. Pour into a glass and enjoy!

Conclusion

Congratulations! You've reached the end of this comprehensive sinusitis and sinusitis diet guide. It's been a journey filled with valuable information, practical tips, and actionable advice. By reading this guide, you've taken an important step in managing your sinusitis through dietary changes, and that's truly commendable.

Sinusitis can be challenging, but remember, it's not insurmountable. As we've learned, the food we consume plays a significant role in our overall health and well-being, including the state of our sinuses. You now know to make informed decisions about what you eat and how it impacts your condition.

Don't worry if it all seems overwhelming at first. Change is always daunting, but it becomes easier as you go along. Start by gradually incorporating the recommended foods into your diet and observe how your body responds. Keep a food diary if it helps. This can be a useful tool to track your progress and identify any patterns or triggers.

Remember, everyone is different. What works for one person might not work for another. It's okay to experiment and find what best suits you. The ultimate goal here is to alleviate your symptoms, improve your quality of life, and enable you to live comfortably with sinusitis.

Also, don't forget about the importance of hydration. Drinking plenty of water is key in managing sinusitis, as it helps to thin mucus and promote sinus drainage. So, keep that water bottle close!

While diet plays a significant role, it's just one piece of the puzzle. Regular exercise, adequate sleep, stress management, and medical treatment (when necessary) are all equally crucial in managing sinusitis effectively.

As you embark on this journey, remember to be patient with yourself. Dietary changes won't bring overnight results, but with consistency, you will notice improvements over time. Your efforts will pay off, and every small victory is a step towards a healthier you.

Finally, while this guide provides a solid foundation, it's always advisable to consult with your healthcare provider before making significant dietary changes, especially if you have other underlying health conditions. They can provide personalized advice based on your specific needs and circumstances.

In conclusion, sinusitis might be a part of your life, but it doesn't define you. You have the power to influence your health and well-being. With this guide, you're well-equipped to take control of your sinusitis and lead a healthier, more comfortable life.

So here's to you, for taking the initiative, for seeking knowledge, and for striving for better health. Congratulations once again on completing this guide, and good luck on your journey towards managing sinusitis through a balanced diet.

FAQs

What is sinusitis?

Sinusitis is a common condition where the lining of the sinuses becomes inflamed. It's usually caused by a viral infection and often improves within two or three weeks. Symptoms can include a runny or blocked nose, facial pain and tenderness, a high temperature, and a reduced sense of smell.

Can diet affect sinusitis?

Yes, diet can significantly impact sinusitis. Certain foods can cause inflammation and mucus production, which can exacerbate sinusitis symptoms. Conversely, other foods have anti-inflammatory properties that can help alleviate symptoms.

What foods should be avoided with sinusitis?

People with sinusitis are often advised to avoid dairy products, as they can increase mucus production. Other potential triggers include refined sugars, spicy foods, and foods high in histamines, like aged cheeses, fermented foods, and alcohol.

Which foods are beneficial for sinusitis?

Foods rich in antioxidants and anti-inflammatory compounds can be beneficial for sinusitis. This includes fruits and vegetables, lean proteins, whole grains, and healthy fats from sources like avocados and nuts. Hydrating foods and beverages can also help thin out mucus and promote sinus drainage.

Can drinking water help sinusitis?

Absolutely. Staying well-hydrated is essential for those with sinusitis. Water helps to thin the mucus in the nasal passages, allowing it to drain more effectively and reducing congestion.

Should people with sinusitis exercise?

Yes, regular exercise can enhance immune function and circulation, helping to prevent and manage sinusitis. However, during acute sinusitis episodes, intense exercise might exacerbate symptoms. Light activities like walking may be more suitable during these times.

Is it necessary to consult a healthcare provider before changing the diet for sinusitis?

While this guide provides general advice, it's always recommended to consult with a healthcare provider before making significant dietary changes. They can provide personalized advice based on individual health conditions and needs.

References and Helpful Links

GoodRX . (n.d.). https://www.goodrx.com/conditions/sinus-infection/best-foods-to-eat-sinus-infection

Professional, C. C. M. (n.d.-b). Sinus infection (Sinusitis). Cleveland Clinic. https://my.clevelandclinic.org/health/diseases/17701-sinusitis

Acute sinusitis - Symptoms and causes - Mayo Clinic. (2023, August 29). Mayo Clinic. https://www.mayoclinic.org/diseases-conditions/acute-sinusitis/symptoms-causes/syc-20351671

Sinusitis - Types, causes, symptoms, complications and treatment. (2023, October 25). https://www.pacehospital.com/sinusitis-types-causes-symptoms-and-treatment

Admin. (2021, October 6). Remedies and lifestyle modifications to manage sinusitis – Sree Saran Medical Center. https://www.sreesaranmedicalcenter.com/remedies-and-lifestyle-modifications-to-manage-sinusitis/

Sparks, D. (2018, November 27). Home Remedies: Self-help for sinusitis. Mayo Clinic News Network. https://newsnetwork.mayoclinic.org/discussion/home-remedies-self-help-for-sinusitis/

10 foods to avoid when suffering from sinusitis. (2023, August 29). Pristine Care. https://www.pristyncare.com/blog/foods-to-avoid-in-sinusitis/

www.ingramcontent.com/pod-product-compliance
Lightning Source LLC
LaVergne TN
LVHW012034060526
838201LV00061B/4604